F★A★M★O★U★S
ATHLETES

Photo credits:

Allsport—Pages 16, 21
Jonathan Daniel/Allsport—Page 23
Hulton Deutsch/Allsport—Pages 15, 23
Tony Duffy/Allsport—Pages 24-25
Hulton Getty/Allsport—Page 11
Jed Jacobson/Allsport—Page 27
Allan Kaye/Allsport—Page 14
Vincent Laforet/Allsport—Page 14
Ken Levine/Allsport—Pages 22-23
Bob Martin/Allsport—Pages 9, 24-25
James McQuire/Allsport—Page 25
Steve Powell/Allsport—Pages 20, 28, 29
Pascal Rondeau/Allsport—Page 20
Rick Stewart/Allsport—Page 12
Damian Strohmeyer/Allsport—Page 19
AP/Wide World Photos—Cover; End Pages; Pages 6, 7, 8, 9, 10, 11, 12, 13, 14, 15, 16, 17, 18, 19, 20, 21, 22, 24, 27, 28, 29
Corbis-Bettmann—Pages 12, 13, 26-27
UPI/Corbis-Bettmann—Cover; Pages 18, 26, 27, 28
Focus On Sports—Cover
Granger Collection—Page 26

Pages
2-3 and 30-31—
February 23, 1980:
The U.S. Olympic
hockey team celebrates
its thrilling final-round
victory over Finland's
team. It was only the
second time a U.S.
hockey team had
won Olympic
gold.

Visit us at www.kidsbooks.com
Volume discounts available for group purchases.

EYES ON AMERICA™

F★A★M★O★U★S
ATHLETES

Written by
Michael E. Goodman

kidsbooks
Incorporated

WORLDWIDE HEROES

Some of America's most famous athletes are almost as well-known throughout the world as they are in the United States. Fans around the globe cheer their deeds, wear their jerseys, and imitate their styles. These American athletes truly are world champions.

GOLDEN GIRL

Shannon Miller has won more medals than any other American gymnast in history. Shannon won the all-around World Champion title in 1993 and 1994, and two Olympic gold medals in 1996, making her a hero in her hometown of Edmond, Oklahoma— and around the world.

"THE GREATEST"

Muhammad Ali bragged that he was "the Greatest"— then proved it in the boxing ring. He also showed courage when he refused to fight in the Vietnam War and had his heavyweight title taken away. Muhammad won back the championship, earning worldwide admiration. He retired—with the title—in 1979.

ON TOP OF THE WORLD

Michael Jordan was once cut from his high school basketball team. So he worked even harder—and became the NBA's best scorer, defender, and clutch performer. He won the scoring title nine times in 13 years and led the Chicago Bulls to six championships. Kids everywhere want to "be like Mike."

UPER SEVEN

Jackie Joyner-Kersee used er strength, speed, and mping ability in the oughest track contest or women, the hep- athlon. She won lympic gold for hat event in 1988 nd 1992—and the tle of "world's reatest female thlete."

TERRIFIC TARA

Tara Lipinski is only 4'10" and weighs just 82 pounds, but she stood tall to receive the gold medal in women's fig- ure skating at the 1998 Olympics. She won by soaring through seven perfect triple-jump combinations!

CLASS ACT

In 1993, at age 19, Pete Sampras became the youngest man to win the U.S. Open. But success never went to his head. While ranked #1 in the world between 1993 and 1998, Pete gained respect for his sportsmanship *and* his skill.

TOP TIGER

Golf was always a calm sport—until Eldrick "Tiger" Woods came along! After he became the youngest-ever winner of golf's Master's tour- nament (in 1997), millions of young fans began following the sport.

ATHLETES WITH IMPACT

Some American athletes are trailblazers: By their actions on and off the playing field, they have made a difference in sports or the world at large. These athletes have changed the way their sports are played—and, sometimes, how we judge people of a different sex or race.

MIKAN IN THE MIDDLE

George Mikan, 6'10", was the NBA's first famous big man. He planted himself near the basket and tossed in hook after hook to lead the Minneapolis Lakers to five championships between 1949 and 1954.

▲ BEST ALL-AROUND

Native American Jim Thorpe—who excelled in baseball, football, and track—was voted the best all-around American athlete. At the 1912 Olympics, Sweden's king told him: "Sir, you are the greatest athlete in the world." Jim helped form the first pro football league.

SULTAN OF SWAT

George Herman "Babe" Ruth made baseball more exciting by making home runs a common feature of the game. In 1921, he hit 54 homers—more than any entire *team* that year! America's most-popular athlete in the 1920s and 1930s, the Babe may be the best-loved player of all time.

DOING IT ALL

As a child, Mildred Didrikson Zaharias was so good at baseball she was dubbed "Babe," after Babe Ruth. At 18, she won one silver and two gold medals in track and field at the 1932 Olympics. Later, Babe became America's best female golfer—she once won 17 golf tournaments in a row!

EQUAL TO THE TASK

Tennis star Billie Jean King helped prove that female athletes deserve as much fame and fortune as male athletes. In 1973, she won the "Battle of the Sexes" match against male opponent Bobby Riggs, raising public interest in women's sports.

▼ DEFEATING A DICTATOR

Jesse Owens won four gold medals at the 1936 Olympics in Germany—proving that the racist theories of Adolf Hitler and the Nazis were wrong.

BREAKING THE COLOR BARRIER

Until Jackie Robinson joined the Brooklyn Dodgers in 1947, African-American athletes were not allowed to play major-league baseball. Jackie was booed and insulted, but kept his temper—and earned respect. His dignity and skill paved the way for other black athletes to enter pro sports.

BASEBALL'S BEST

Want to create the perfect baseball player? Combine the smooth swing of Ted Williams or Ken Griffey Jr., the amazing accuracy of Greg Maddux or Sandy Koufax, the grace of Joe DiMaggio, and the reflexes of Brooks Robinson or Ozzie Smith!

◀ EYES ON THE PRIZE

Ted Williams played 19 seasons with the Boston Red Sox and hit over .300 in 18 of them. "The Splendid Splinter" also whacked 521 career homers. In 1941, he batted over .400—something that no one has done since.

▶ K FOR KOUFAX

It is appropriate that Koufax begins with a K—the baseball scorers' symbol for a strikeout. When Sandy Koufax took the mound in the 1960s, he mowed batters down with his blazing fastball and sharp-breaking curve. The three-time Cy Young Award winner pitched four no-hitters, including a perfect game.

▲ "JUNIOR"

Throughout the 1990s, amazed fans watched Ken Griffey Jr. power balls high over the outfield wall or make amazing plays in the outfield. Many people consider "Junior" the best all-around player in baseball.

10

◄ A WINNING SECRET

Greg Maddux is the only pitcher to win four Cy Young Awards in a row. He describes the secret of his success as the five Cs: confidence, concentration, consistency, control of every pitch, and change of speeds.

SUPER STREAK

Joe DiMaggio's streak of hitting safely in 56 straight games may be baseball's hardest record to break. It has stood since 1941! "The Yankee Clipper" led his team to the World Series in 10 of his 13 years with the Yankees.

THE WIZARD

Ozzie Smith seldom hit for a high average and almost never hit home runs, but any manager would have loved to have "the Wizard of Oz" on his team. Baseball's best-fielding shortstop, Ozzie earned 13 straight Gold Glove Awards.

Brooks Robinson won 16 consecutive Gold Gloves for his outstanding fielding ability. His glove seemed to be a magnet for any ground ball hit his way.

11

BASEBALL'S HALL OF FAME

According to legend, baseball was first played in Cooperstown, New York, in 1839. That's why the National Baseball Hall of Fame and Museum was built there 100 years later. Millions of visitors have enjoyed seeing plaques and other exhibits that honor baseball's best players.

THE CYCLONE

Denton "Cy" Young retired in 1911 with a record 511 major-league wins (and a record 315 losses). Each year, an award named for Cy Young is given to the best pitcher in each league.

TY'S TWO SIDES

No player in baseball history comes close to Ty Cobb's .367 career batting average, and he is one of only two players to record 4,000 hits. But Ty was nasty on the field: He loved to slide hard into a base—with his sharpened spikes aimed at the opposing fielder.

NEW KID IN THE HALL

Mike Schmidt's 1995 induction into the Hall of Fame celebrated his 548 career homers and 10 Gold Gloves as the National League's best-fielding third baseman.

12

NO DAYS OFF

One day in 1925, the Yankees' first baseman asked to take a day off, so rookie Lou Gehrig was sent in to replace him. Lou was so good, he didn't leave the lineup for 14 years! "The Pride of the Yankees" played in 2,130 consecutive games.

"HAMMERIN' HANK"

Babe Ruth's 714 career home runs was a record that many people thought unbreakable. But in 1974, Henry (Hank) Aaron sent homer #715 into the bullpen. "Hammerin' Hank" set a new record of 755 career homers. He also holds records for runs batted in, extra-base hits, and total bases.

"THE SAY-HEY KID" ▶

Willie Mays had superb baseball skills: He was first-rate at hitting, running, catching, and throwing. He is one of only two players (Henry Aaron is the other) with career totals of more than 3,000 hits and more than 600 home runs.

20-20

For pitchers, winning 20 games in a season is a special feat. Walter Johnson did it for 10 seasons in a row! His roaring fastball earned him the nickname "the Big Train." His career strikeout record stood for more than 50 years.

WINNING ATTITUDE

Bob Gibson combined speed with accuracy—and a bit of a mean streak. Batters knew that he would throw the ball hard and inside if they stood too close to the plate. His 1968 1.12 ERA was the lowest-ever for a pitcher with at least 300 innings pitched.

13

RECORD BREAKERS

Some sports records take many years to set, while others are estab lished in just a few seconds. Either way, record-setting athletes have proven that they are truly the best in their sports—at least till the record gets broken

RYAN'S EXPRESS

Nolan Ryan's fastball was not only tough to hit, it was hard to see. He could pitch a ball 100 miles per hour—or faster! The only pitcher to record more than 5,000 career strikeouts, he also tossed a record seven no-hitters.

"FLO JO"

In 1988, Florence Joyner Griffith became the first American woman to win four medals at one Olympics: three golds and a silver. "Flo Jo" was daz- zlingly fast—her speed was once clocked at 23.5 miles per hour!

Jerry Rice is the only receiver in NFL history to catch more than 1,000 passes during his career.

THE MAC & SAMMY SHOW

In 1998, two sluggers blasted past a record that had stood for 37 years: 61 home runs in a single season. Mark McGwire (*left*) hit 70 homers—the new record—and Sammy Sosa (*right*) hit 66!

14

SPITZ BLITZ

Mark Spitz won gold *and* set a world record in all seven races he swam at the 1972 Olympics. Add his triumphs in the 1968 Games, and he has a whopping nine gold medals—matched only by track star Carl Lewis.

▼ REACH FOR THE SKY

Kareem Abdul-Jabbar's 7'2" height and amazing touch helped make him the NBA's all-time leader in scoring, shots blocked, and games played. He led teams to six NBA titles.

▼ On September 20, 1998, Cal Ripken sat out a game—breaking his streak of consecutive games played. His record, which stands at 2,632, is probably unbreakable.

▲ DANDY DAN

Dan Marino's strong arm and lightning-fast delivery kept the Miami Dolphins in the swim in the 1980s. His name tops NFL lists for all-time leaders in pass attempts, completions, passing yardage, and touchdown passes.

BASKETBALL'S COURT MAGICIANS

THE BIG "O" ▶
Over the 1961-1962 season, Oscar Robertson averaged a "triple-double": 30.8 points, 12.5 rebounds, and 11.4 assists. It was the only time that has been done in NBA history!

Basketball was invented by a gym teacher in Springfield, Massachusetts, in 1892. Its popularity has been spreading around the world ever since.

"LARRY LEGEND"
Larry Bird's shooting, rebounding, and passing skills led the Celtics to three NBA titles in the 1980s, earning him the nickname "Larry Legend." In 1997, he became coach of the Indiana Pacers—and was named the NBA's best coach in his rookie season.

TRIPLE FIGURES ▲
Most professional basketball teams find it tough to score 100 points in a game. During one contest in 1962, however, Wilt "the Stilt" Chamberlain scored that many points all by himself! One season, he averaged more than 50 points and 25 rebounds a game.

At 6'1", point guard
John Stockton is short
by NBA standards,
but he stands tall as
the NBA's all-time
leader in assists
and steals.

MAGIC TOUCH

After watching
Earvin Johnson
outscore, out-rebound,
and outpass every
other player during a
high school game, a
sportswriter dubbed
him "Magic." Magic's
greatest trick was
winning games. He
led the L.A. Lakers to
five NBA champion-
ships in the 1980s.

PICTURE PERFECT

A few years ago, the NBA
decided to use a silhouette of
the "perfect" basketball player
for its logo. They chose Jerry
West. Jerry's picture-perfect
jump shot and skillful ball
handling helped him become
an NBA All-Star in each of his
14 years in the league.

DEE-FENSE! ▶

Bill Russell was a
master at blocking shots
and getting opponents off-
balance. The five-time MVP
led the Boston Celtics to 11
NBA titles in 13 years. In
1968, he became the
NBA's first African-
American coach.

FOOTBALL'S FINEST

It takes toughness to survive on the gridiron. From Bronko Nagurski in the 1930s (*left*) to Barry Sanders in the 1990s (*right*), the finest professional football players have had to be quick *and* powerful. That combination of speed and strength has made pro football a favorite among American sports fans for more than 75 years.

◀ Bronko Nagurski starred in both offense and defense for the Chicago Bears—and led the Bears to championships in 1932 and 1933.

Barry Sanders, who started his pro career in 1989, rushed for 1,000 or more yards a season for nine seasons in a row—and counting. ▶

TD MASTER

Pro teams seldom threw passes. Then Don Hutson joined the Green Bay Packers in 1935—and caught an 83-yard touchdown pass to lead the way to a 7-0 victory. His career record of 99 touchdown passes stood for more than 50 years.

"JOHNNY U" ▶

Drafted by the Pittsburgh Steelers but cut before the season started, Johnny Unitas signed as backup quarterback with the Baltimore Colts. He quickly won the starting job—and steered the team to NFL championships in 1958 and 1959. Johnny holds the record for consecutive games with at least one touchdown pass: 47!

For nine years (1957-1965), Jim Brown (#32 *above*) was the dominant running back in the NFL. He gained an average of 5.2 yards each time he carried the ball—and never missed a game. He is considered the best running back ever.

18

MONTANA MAGIC
During Joe Montana's NFL career (1979-1994), he quarterbacked the San Francisco 49ers to four Super Bowl wins. He retired with records for most consecutive passes completed (22) and most consecutive games with 300 or more yards passing (5).

▲ THE ANGRY MAN
Before a game, Dick Butkus would think of things that made him mad—then take his anger out on opposing blockers and runners! He was voted the best (and meanest) middle linebacker of all time.

▲ "SWEETNESS"
Any defensive player who tried to tackle Walter Payton might find it hard to believe that his nickname was "Sweetness." He had the speed to outrun tacklers on wide sweeps and the strength to go up the middle. In 1984, he became the NFL's career rushing leader.

COOL IN THE CLUTCH

Some athletes thrive on pressure, performing best when time is running out or when one final, superhuman effort is needed to turn defeat into victory.

GRACE UNDER PRESSURE

Diver Greg Louganis completed more than 200,000 dives in practice and competition. None was more difficult than his last. At the 1988 Olympics, he performed a perfect reverse 3 1/2 somersault to come from behind and win his fourth gold medal.

TEN TIMES TWO

Mary Lou Retton was in second place in the women's all-around gymnastics championship at the 1984 Olympics. To take first, she had to score two perfect tens. She did—and became the first-ever female U.S. gymnast to earn a gold medal.

▲ "MR. OCTOBER"

Reggie Jackson seemed to play best in postseason contests. On October 18, 1977, he smacked home runs in three straight at-bats to help the New York Yankees win the World Series.

WEE WILLIE

Willie Shoemaker had ridden more than 8,000 winners during his horse-racing career, but no one expected another at the 1986 Kentucky Derby. At 54, Willie was older than the other jockeys, and his horse was not considered to be the fastest. But Willie coaxed Ferdinand from last place to first, and won America's most-famous horse race.

BLAZING PEDALS

After cycling more than 2,000 miles in the 1989 Tour de France race, Greg LeMond was in second place. He pedaled the last 17 miles in less than 27 minutes to win by the closest margin ever: eight seconds!

HIS CROWNING GLORY

Game 7 of the 1960 World Series between the Pittsburgh Pirates and the New York Yankees. Bottom of the ninth. Score tied 9-9. Bill Mazeroski at bat. With one mighty swing, the Pirates' second baseman sent a rocket over the left-field wall, giving the Pirates a 10-9 win and the Series crown!

◀ "THE COMEBACK KID"

Quarterback John Elway has directed his team to 37 comeback victories! In 1998, he led the underdog Denver Broncos to their first Super Bowl victory, over the heavily favored Green Bay Packers.

GOING FOR THE GOLD

For America's finest amateur athletes, there is no feeling greater than hearing "The Star-Spangled Banner" played to honor a gold-medal performance. Over the years, American Olympians have proven that they are among the world's best athletes.

◀ SHINING STAR

Picabo Street's daredevil skiing style helped make her one of America's most popular athletes. *Picabo* is an American Indian word that means "shining waters." She certainly shone at the 1998 Winter Olympics, taking the gold in the women's super grand slalom.

JUST LIKE JESSE

When Carl Lewis was a boy, his father told him how Jesse Owens won four gold medals at the 1936 Olympics. In 1984, Carl matched that feat—in the same four events! Only swimmer Mark Spitz has matched Lewis's Olympic total of nine gold medals.

A TOUGH TEN

The decathlon's 10 track-and-field events take two days to complete, but getting ready takes years.

Bruce Jenner practiced running, jumping, and throwing for eight hours a day, 365 days a year. That earned him gold at the 1976 Games—and the title of "world's best all-around athlete."

Janet Evans, America's finest longest-distance swimmer, won four gold medals at the 1988 and 1992 Olympics.

FOUR IN A ROW

Discus thrower Al Oerter won gold medals at the 1956 and 1960 Olympics. In 1964, he won his third gold medal *and* broke an Olympic record—despite back and rib injuries. He won a fourth gold in 1968 with another record toss.

BONNIE THE BLUR

When speed skater Bonnie Blair lacked the money for training and travel expenses, the police department in her hometown of Champaign, Illinois, raised the funds. In 1994, she paid them back by winning five Winter Olympics gold medals—the most ever by an American woman.

DOUBLE TIME

Some runners specialize in dashes: 100- or 200-meter events. Others focus on 400- and 800-meter events, which require endurance as well as speed. In 1996, Michael Johnson became the only man to win gold in the 200- and 400-meter Olympic races—and set a new world record in the 200-meter.

23

HOT ON ICE

Every four years, millions of Americans cheer on U.S. skaters at the Winter Olympics. American skaters are usually among the medalists, and American women have taken home gold more often than those of any other country.

STAGE FRIGHT

Dorothy Hamill, the 1976 Olympic gold medalist, had severe stage fright. When she began skating, however, the nervousness vanished and was replaced by energy and elegance. Dorothy invented a spin known as the "Hamill camel."

TOP FORM

In 1948, Dick Button became America's first Olympic-gold winner in skating. In 1952, he made the first successful triple jump in Olympic competition—and won his second-straight gold.

GOLDEN GIRL

Californian Michelle Kwan has won two world championships and an Olympic silver. She is favored to win gold at the 2002 Olympics.

JUMPING TO GLORY

When Brian Boitano took his first skating lesson at age 8, his teacher noticed that he could spin three times faster than any other student. Brian became a prize-winning skater. At the 1988 Olympics, he did his original ""Tano triple lutz" and six other triples perfectly—and took home the gold.

ALWAYS DREAM

Kristi Yamaguchi's warmth and grace helped her become world and Olympic champ in the 1990s. She's a hero off the ice, too: She established the Always Dream Foundation, which supports organizations having a positive influence on American children.

PERFECT PAIR

Pairs skaters must show their individual skills, yet blend perfectly with a partner. Tai Babilonia and Randy Gardner did that in 1979—and became the first U.S. pair in 29 years to win the world championship.

BALLERINA ON ICE

Peggy Fleming's great loves were skating and ballet. She combined the two in competition, enchanting spectators and judges alike. Her elegance on the ice made the difficult combinations she performed look simple and smooth.

CHAMPS IN THE RING

Boxers first competed in Greece in 688 B.C. The sport was brought to America by British settlers, and has thrived here ever since. U.S. boxers have always dominated the heavyweight championships.

▼ "THE BROWN BOMBER"

Joe Louis held the world heavyweight title for more than 11 years. From 1937 to 1948, he defeated 25 different challengers! "The Brown Bomber" was the first African-American athlete to become a hero to both white and black Americans.

◄ "THE BOSTON STRONG BOY"

When John L. Sullivan won the heavyweight title in 1892, he became America's first great sports hero. "The Boston Strong Boy" went from town to town, offering $1,000 to any challenger who could fight him for four rounds. Few made it past the *first* round! He was boxing's last bare-knuckle champion.

"MANASSA MAULER"

Jack Dempsey (*at right*) won 25 fights in the first round, and once knocked out an opponent just four seconds into the match! He was heavyweight champ from 1919 to 1927.

GETTING A CHANCE ▶

Jack Johnson was a great boxer, but he had trouble getting a chance to win the heavyweight crown: Most top boxers refused to fight a black opponent. He finally got his chance, and became champ in 1908.

ALL-AROUND CHAMP

Evander Holyfield, heavyweight champion for most of the 1990s, earned the nickname "the Real Deal" because of his boxing skills in the ring and his calm personality and honesty outside it.

▲ SWEET VICTORY

He was born Walker Smith, but fought under the name Ray Robinson. After a reporter called his style "sweet as sugar," he was known as "Sugar Ray." Sugar Ray Robinson was the welterweight boxing champ from 1946 to 1951, then won five titles as a middleweight.

Rocky Marciano is the only professional boxing champion to go undefeated during his career. "The Rock" was 49-0 when back problems forced him to retire in 1956.

27

TOPS IN TENNIS

Tennis was born in England, but was soon adopted by Americans. The International Tennis Hall of Fame in Rhode Island honors many Americans—from Beals Wright of the 1910s to Chris Evert of the 1980s.

UNMATCHED

Helen Wills Moody dominated women's tennis. She won her first U.S. championship in 1923 at age 18, and the last of her eight Wimbledon crowns in 1938. In 1928 and 1929, she won the French, Wimbledon, and U.S. championships without losing a single set!

TRAILBLAZER

Althea Gibson is remembered as the first African-American tennis champion. She won the Wimbledon *and* U.S. championships in 1957 and 1958, and was named America's Outstanding Woman Athlete.

SUPER, BUT HOW?

John McEnroe was known for showing two things on the tennis court: skill and bad temper. In the late 1970s, reporters nicknamed him "Super Brat," but a fellow tennis pro called him "the kind of player the world might see only once every 50 years."

FANTASTIC FOUR

Don Budge won the Australian, U.S., Wimbledon, and French championships all in the same year (1938)! He was the first player to capture all four events—known as the Grand Slam—and no male player has done it since.

Jimmy Connors' mother once told him, "If you want to play tennis, play hard." He took her advice: His aggressive style won him a career-record 109 men's singles tournaments. He was ranked first, second, or third in the world from 1973 to 1984.

KING ARTHUR

Arthur Ashe was the first African-American male to triumph at the U.S. Open (1968) and Wimbledon (1975). He became a driving force for change, encouraging young African Americans to compete in tennis—and to strive for success in all walks of life.

◀ QUIET CHRIS

Chris Evert had a quiet, reserved personality, but there was no tougher competitor on the court. During her 19 years as a pro, she never ranked lower than fourth in the world. She won 18 Grand Slam event titles, including six U.S. Open championships.